murmurations

Anthony
Thomas
Lombardi

murmurations

poems

Anthony
Thomas
Lombardi

table of contents

self-portrait as murmuration   1

fragments from Amy Winehouse's stepwork journal   9
& with every sunrise another reason to mourn   10
i think i'm finally ready to admit that i don't know the first thing about forgiveness   11
spent gladiator #3   12
through the front window of a haunted house, Amy Winehouse remembers
the sky, a bruise   13

fragments from Amy Winehouse's stepwork journal   17
moral inventory sonnet featuring the serenity prayer   18
on Lisa "Left Eye" Lopes's stay in rehab & why i still sing to the dead   19
ghosts in the studio where Amy Winehouse abandons her comeback album   21

fragments from Amy Winehouse's stepwork journal   23
ode to the luna moth & my psychiatrist who warns me lithium will shorten my lifespan   24
dirge for the last night of Eric Dolphy's life, part I   26
preparing for the next ice age while Amy Winehouse plays solitaire   27

fragments from Amy Winehouse's stepwork journal   31
relapse dream   32
moral inventory   33
ode to the seagull with what looks like a chicken bone in its beak but could be
another seagull's leg for all i know   34
on her first tour sober Amy Winehouse plays nothing but ballads & refuses to sing
anything in past tense   36

fragments from Amy Winehouse's stepwork journal	39
taste of cherries	40
i can think of a dozen different ways to break that Motown 12" & none of them will sound as sweet as "Dancing in the Street"	42
moral inventory	44
grief	45
fragments from Amy Winehouse's stepwork journal	51
DMX teaches me how to pray	52
aubade with Nina Simone who sang "Sinnerman" & the whole world lost its balance	54
nature retreat nocturne with Amy Winehouse	60
fragments from Amy Winehouse's stepwork journal	63
on why Miles Davis quit playing ballads	64
dirge for the last night of Eric Dolphy's life, part II	68
all my attempts at meditation end in shouting matches with ghosts	69
last night i turned off the pilot light	70
fragments from Amy Winehouse's stepwork journal	73
arguing with my sponsor's ghost about the last place i saw him alive	74
the night of Dexter Gordon's comeback	76
that winter i wrote the same poem over & over	77
upon hearing Prince sing "Purple Rain" at First Avenue in Minneapolis in 1983, i begin to understand my mother's love life	79
fragments from Amy Winehouse's stepwork journal	83
my beloved forgets how to pray	84
the summer after DMX died every rainfall felt like a benediction	86
God loves everybody, don't remind me	87
withdrawal dream with Amy Winehouse chain-smoking in the dining hall of a rehabilitation center & plotting her escape	88

fragments from Amy Winehouse's stepwork journal	93
i am having so much fun without you	94
on Whitney Houston's acceptance speech at the 2001 BET Awards & why i pray in the dark	97
i admit it i've never seen a falling star	99
unholy	100
delays & departures in an airport bar with Amy Winehouse	102
fragments from Amy Winehouse's stepwork journal	105
slow singing & flower bringing	106
The Truth	108
the profits of gravity	109
the ocean isn't haunted it just holds our dead	111
fragments from Amy Winehouse's stepwork journal	115
on Survivor's Guilt ending with "Ruff Ryders' Anthem" by DMX	116
one side of Amy Winehouse's first post-rehab interview	118
ouroboros	119
on the gruesome death of honeybees, Sonny Rollins's sabbatical & other incentives for loneliness	120
self-portrait as murmuration	123

murmurations © 2025 by Anthony Thomas Lombardi

NO AI TRAINING: Without in any way limiting the author's exclusive rights under copyright, any use of this publication to "train" generative artificial intelligence (AI) technologies to generate text is expressly prohibited. The author reserves all rights to license uses of this work for generative AI training and development of machine learning language models.

Photography by Savannah Lauren
Cover and Interior Design: Alex Bruce
Project Lead: KMA Sullivan

ISBN: 978-1-946303-03-5
Printed in the United States of America

Published by YesYes Books
1631 NE Broadway St #121
Portland, OR 97232
YesYesBooks.com

KMA Sullivan, Publisher
Karah Kemmerly, Managing Editor
Gale Marie Thompson, Senior Editor
Devin Devine, Assistant Editor
Jill Kolongowski, Manuscript Copy Editor
James Sullivan, Assistant Editor

for Scott & Rob

*& anyone still wrestling
with their angels*

*I had nothing
and I was still changed.
Like a costume, my numbness
was taken away. Then
hunger was added.*

LOUISE GLÜCK

The end of the world must be just ahead.

ARTHUR RIMBAUD

self-portrait as murmuration

my first memory is my four limbs
        the expanse of a school bus door.

    my throat charred
           cardinal red, gurgling

        almost carnal
               no one heard

            as loudly as my mother.
      she cried. i cried first.

           ▽

        through every project courtyard a mother's mouth
swarms the streets: *shut up* or *come home*.

this does not make clear whether the windows
                are open or closed. i am too young

           to know any space small enough
                    to contain me. my mouth

           holds rain like streets
                   full of holes.

                      ▽

                    after a storm, birds will sing. having kept
            spirit & body bound, they regale the night

            with their ablutions. swollen soil will cast
                        its pheromones into the air.

                                        there is a word for this, a scent
                        so loud my palms leave

                                welts on my ears. there is a psalm
                that lingers: *Let there be none*

                        to extend mercy unto him.
        in the grave it will be quiet.

                        ▽

                my first memory is my skin
scaling seasons. it's dark & hell

is cold. my first words are
                where are the starlings? even the pigeons

                are sparse. light-starved limbs
                                silhouette the wall, pale

                        imitations of pale fists. a fissure
                        revises the sky

                        but no one smells smoke. only ashes
                        fall, little fine feathers.

                                ▽

                        heaved from hell, i shiver
                                like a cursed star. i am quiet

                                enough to feel my teeth curve,
                chatter. my mother's hands are as big as God's

                        green thumb. the hyacinths are brimming
                with honeybees. i pluck them

                    harmless. i fit, sheathed
           right between my mother's

              index finger & thumb, red
& slumped as a baby's knee.

       ▽

my first memory is arriving.
        home still looks like home—

     cubs crawl the walls then bruise
          their tailbones, each effort to slip

            out, a slow slide, solitary, little wolf prints
                paws softened from spit

                leaving spoor: patterns of failed flight
                    across hardwood floors. a fistful of my hair

                    legs dragged, charred, on the carpet. maybe
                      i'm wrong about the stars. maybe

                      they're blessed. maybe God
                          has been using the floor as an ashtray

                        by floor, i mean sky. by the sky
                  my back is straight as a cutting board.

                    in the basement, cave cold, i pluck
        the needles from the top of the washing machine

              blood blackened at their tips
    treaded & truer than the gospel.

       ▽

      my first memory is a murmuration
somewhere between Georgia

                  & Florida. traveling with my mother's
boyfriend, who drives a rig up the coast

        she tells me now, grown
into whatever body would have me

that he hated me, made cruelty
              a faux pas, like being caught at a party

                  with a pocket full of hors d'oeuvres.
                               when summer inspires mercury
                                     to cry *mercy*, i see a woman break

                                    her stride to greet a breeze with raised arms
                                        & a *Hallelujah*. the word hangs

                                    like a baited lure. the taste of metal
                                    swims in my mouth

                                    for a week. i remember
                              his Portuguese accent—how it snagged

                              & snared, daring me to change
                      ablution to *ablation*

                          a snip, a crescent so small
                you can't feel a thing. then the back

                    cab of his truck, cutting out my tongue
with a butter knife

                when he'd watched me make of my right hand
a bayonet.

            ▽

                  the starlings billow at dusk
the horizon a slit in a damson

dangling, a daydream in the bathroom
      mirror, a slip.

    with a single fingertip
        i can paint an ocean.

        my first memory is heartbreak after rain.
            watching worms rise from dirt

            disoriented by light, drawn to it.
                the birds sing here, too.

                a summons
                    that dinner is served.

                    ▽

                the last time i told a truth my mother asked me
                    where it hurts. i smear

                the bleeding ink
                    here   *here*   *here*   i don't say

                  she doesn't hear. i point
              to the starling's swarm, the moon

              swallowed & she's looking at the crescent
on my fingernail.

                  ▽

            my first memory is sainthood
        granted on the gallows.

i haven't remembered anything since.

To love the hibiscus,
you must first love the monsoon

HALA ALYAN

For these dead birds sigh a prayer.

WILLIAM SHAKESPEARE

step one

fragments from Amy Winehouse's stepwork journal

under a cold cherry moon i pour myself parallel. shrugged out of enough beds content with near any floor. i kick my legs free, cover my head like weather, like carpet burn. remember the hotel room, a joke of paradise. the mess of glasses & shot nerves our shirts slick with what a body refuses licking my heels. morning found me, a hard break, all but breathing. the birds were so silent they disappeared. remember drowning then lose my jeans, long goodbyes, hearts with strings—anything that will pull me under. hold smoke in my hand. remember warmth between the rain.

& with every sunrise another reason to mourn

in church basements i upstaged the old-timers   my mouth a moon
        -less cave & an orchid tucked   behind my ear
when i qualified with my own   story i couldn't remember
        half of it told instead   the legend of the huma bird
who never alighted on land   or branch spent its years in flight
        wings lithe & torrential   as a piano's bent arpeggio
now i remember too well the trail   of nails like hollow points palms
        leaking rust ancient christians   called an anxious heart
the 8th deadly sin   a shark keeps its pulse for an hour after it stops
        swimming then gets picked apart   by schools of fish
or so said the nurse when i sat in a hospital   piss pink with blood
        & a twitch in my chest   i've been scrubbing my hands
skinless ever since   push my face up to my face
        in the window   where black-crowned herons drift
as if poured from a bucket   so thin & saintly it feels voyeuristic
        to look   i've been stealing glances at disappearing things
since my lips could hold their spit   my beloved's back
        its narrow march   a star's shadow   now i only swipe
the severed grapes from fruit stands   allow wasps to sail undisturbed
        around my head   lose myself in strobes of warmth
            that bleed through endless clouds
        i know they call this grace   it's the mercy i can't take

i think i'm finally ready to admit that i don't know the first thing about forgiveness

once i wandered in penance   the only souls still around
a small band of ghosts   who stretched their legs
on a sunless veranda   rattling a tune with jars
full of teeth   i plucked petals off pale tulips
heard the same song in *she loves me not*
& *can this kill me*
                      for years i'd steal every vessel from its siren
pick the matchwood out of my throat   with fingernails thick
as nickels   i made no distinction   between powder that soothes
a baby's gums   & powder that puts down tameless broncos
when i tottered into detox   the intake nurse didn't bother
to break her eyes from my chart   *with a heartbeat like that, it's a miracle you're still alive*
                      it's no wonder i see desire
the way it looks in cartoons   hyenas walk upright   as charmed
as you or i by a parrot's speech   coyotes with tongues like runways
never catch their prey & nobody starves   even pigeons dumb
with hunger   barrel into glass & get rewarded
with crowns full of stars
                      in lieu of apologies i've learned to sing
a sound so solemn   passing strangers stop to leave spare pennies
on my eyes   but the pigeons just crane their necks & peck themselves
godless   pavement flecked with little red florets   the heart pumps & pumps

spent gladiator #3

sundown, a closed door borrows your reflection

an assortment of notes submerged in the black
slate of cold glass. your fingers come together
as something molten, magic. play dead

& the shattered image reassembles. on the shoreline

where i made tourniquets of white flags, you
evanesced like an ocean eating sand. i, too,
have circled the drain, beat anyone to my own punch

to save face. in a dream, a boxing match flickers like film

stuck in a projector: the pummeled fighter staggers, past
the point of trying. once, i let a feral animal claw
my face, a ferocity i refused to disrupt. what did i miss

in the fable of the field mouse who scuttled into a foxhole

& emerged unscathed? there's a comfort in growing weary
of resistance: baring raw gums & yawning as some saint
dances strobelights into eyes drawn shut.

gloves unlaced, my mouthguard sings the dead alive.

through the front window of a haunted house,
Amy Winehouse remembers the sky, a bruise

for centuries nostalgia was considered a disease
from the Greek *nostos*, a longing
to return. you follow the moon
here, ghostly in the morning,
but even that is a reflection
of a reflection.
you kick some rubble & watch it soar,
recall the slow tumble, how your skin swelled
& turned like summer fruit.
you vowed you'd only bend your knees
for God but once you loved a mortal man
& down you went.
when the sky took him it spat
back the bones stripped bare & holy.
God spared no mercy. even now
there's salt stuck to your shoulder
& you can't so much as wet your lips
without the beat of locust wings.
heaven is full
of hungry streets. even the stars
are famished. this you catch
in the mirror's kiss
where objects are closer than they appear
—the sorrow in sainthood so choking
you throw open the window
that holds back a sky almost criminal.
craving a sign or a song
of relic, you place your ear
to the walls & floor
but silence flows like quicksand.
the sun starts to rise, slipping out
from behind the squat

all bedecked with mourning doves.
you can't take your eyes off of them
already feeling their flight. but grief
is for the living & another miracle
isn't in you. you open your mouth
to sing them home but only dust
comes out.

step two

fragments from Amy Winehouse's stepwork journal

rounding every empty lot for hours i must have walked straight past the place a hundred times—a house hidden behind years of green growth gone brown. as long as they know i have nothing left to give up i'm willing to sit still. i'm sick enough when my hands act the role of God-fearing across my chest every time i pass a holy house, like the shame burning my skin is only there to pacify fire, the debts i owe, waiting for me below. somehow i ended up down a flight of stairs, one you need to trust in *something* if you want to meet the floor. at the end a sanctuary pressed between bricks bathed in pale blue light. against any kind of sense of self-control i swam in its shadows, played marriage with the wall, close as i could get to spilled warmth without touching. my hands, caned, wouldn't grip together when i tried to sing. *keep God by the bed.* i held odds like chips off the shoulder, rolled down my sleeves, played the shots long or dead.

moral inventory sonnet featuring the serenity prayer

only now do i—a full grown man—recognize
the violence that lives in praise: the feral dance
that erupts from bones, possessed, while i try to kill
a roach. surveilling the refuge beneath my bed, its frame
raised on crates, i curse the ground that's close enough
to kiss. i plead with my cat to earn his keep—he's of no
help whatever—my mattress, suddenly, a rostrum.
but i'm in no place to lead: my pagan life is threatened
by a spindly copper pest. i shout-whisper to the ceiling
the serenity prayer plying my tongue, a split oar
to invoke a bloodless conquest. my cat, too, is crying
for relief—from hunger, heat, or the varmint, now
at hard-won peace, i can't tell. i lean my head against
cool tiles, burning *O Lord, find me—discover me like fire.*

on Lisa "Left Eye" Lopes's stay in rehab & why i still sing to the dead

a woman steps into a body
of water. her own
choosing. torrential wind

kicks the brown lake
out of her. of course
she's still breathing.

you know they're waiting
in the wings but you're doing
your thing. when you awake

fresh as forests
you'll spill fire—
set waterfalls

aflame. the bathtub is filled
with jewels.
whichever sparkle

is worth your bearing
you'll soak
in fluids

sweet as mud.
calf-deep in a pool
of cuttlefish.

sometimes rainbows don't
belong to us. on soft nights
you sing their colors

& they're summonable:
cerulean. magnolia.
car crash.

sometimes religion
is only a graze, a gift
still dripping with God's

rosewater. calendula tied
to your wrist like blood
pressure: eternal baptism.

papavers still
burning but you're bent
on picking them anyway.

ghosts in the studio where Amy Winehouse
abandons her comeback album

what is it they say?
that the voice is a vessel?

look. you already know that. God spoke
through fluorescence & gauze & songs

rose like Lazarus, spilled when the sun hung fat
bleaching walls through London smog.

now wet leaves slide down windows
cutting shapes of dusk who shadowbox

in corners piled high with broken pulpits
your breath still warm over blackened wicks.

what is it they want from you?
to know that you still crave?

the moon is a sliver
sunk into the sky's flesh.

you're inconsolable.
the sun won't be back until morning.

step three

fragments from Amy Winehouse's stepwork journal

guilt, like luck or false gods, don't just appear on your shoulder in a puff of smoke. it's that night in Brixton rewriting history to game my own memory. it's angling my face through the lighting at gigs to hide tears i'd sworn had worn down to scars. i've earned this role. i'm a bloody cheat—always riding ships too far past the sunset, ignoring the birds who try to keep me on track when the rocks are singing my name. who was playing lookout in the lighthouse, shining that lonely shade of blue deep into midnight? my friends who aren't dying are already dead. now i lay myself down for a new man who parts the clouds with His hands & makes ships from refuse & i'm just one more animal safe from the flood.

ode to the luna moth & my psychiatrist who warns me lithium will shorten my lifespan

i am foolish about so much—a half-hearted *maybe*
will rouse me to rub wishes into moth wings, warm my hands over
votives lit for i can't tell the dead or still dying, crush five fingers
of a rocks glass. you get it—i'm addicted
to feeling. are you not set aflush by the gall of a streetlight
mimicking the moon? who wouldn't mimic the moon? i have
mimicked the moon. instead of casting a copper glow over
lovers i gingerly carried coal into churches
swallowed by smoke. i was the classical music
that plays at Port Authority, a pistol
itchy on a June night. the night was almost day
when i caught sight of how i'll look
when i'm old—eyes viper black, crusted dribble
like a string of burnt rosary beads, a mutiny
of stars defacing my arms. i nearly shrieked
myself mute. look. the world is on fire, the stars
are necessary. a bartender once called me
unkeepupwithable & i wore it as a badge
before my liver began to glare, spectacles
hugging the tip of its nasal bridge. look.
i walk around my house where i live alone
tangled in paltry thread-count cotton
with my eyes chewed out. you see how i said *house*?
it isn't a house. you see how i said *ghost*? i'm ill
-fitted & easily swayed & have my breath held
captive. don't look now. a luna moth is landing
on the nape of your neck, his wingspan close
to devotional. he soars to meet his mate
through a summer ripe with midnights knowing
not even the pleasures of a tongue.
once she lay eggs, he will die. starved
for his namesake, he sails past a streetlight

with the Eye of Horus painted on each wing
their flicker in cadence with the bulb
in the night sky, a blur burning bright
before their soft betrayal. look—
you can look up now.

dirge for the last night of Eric Dolphy's life, part I

the needle's glint harsh against the porcelain of the bathroom sink: the difference between what I'm told & what is coming to define my relationship with the truth. years later I'm still using silk & bone to stitch my wounds. once my aunt asked me to piss in a cup for her— stuttered something about the time toxins take to escape your body only she didn't say toxins. during my own stay in detox, I carefully count seconds between shallow breaths. I've seen my grandmother, hands steady as stone, prick blood from her finger, sink medication into her skin, & already I'm considering the depth of my deluge.

preparing for the next ice age while Amy Winehouse plays solitaire

> *Fear, poverty, alcoholism, loneliness are terminal illnesses. Emergencies, in fact.*
> LUCIA BERLIN

you match kings & spades, queens
    & clovers while my knees groan
on wood grain where I seal

    splitting planks. I've known hunger
to crawl through slivers that starved
    rooms of light, tongues so ripe

they'd rot in the arctic. on streets dazed
    in dim light I'd sell out
any lover who stanched my blood

    where folks would kill
for a warmth this lonely.
    when was the last time you felt

a wrist flutter, the beat of blood
    that wasn't your own?
when we gathered our stockpile

    the man at the bodega who played
a sonata with the keychain
    in his pocket brushed your arm

when he passed back your change.
    word from the block: he still sleeps
with his late wife, an heiress

        who spat diamonds with her hand
on the throne. I wonder if Queen Anne
        ever took a common lover

riding steeds beneath crimson
        skies, their handkerchiefs billowing
into hard-won dusk. even bees, gifting us

        the blush of her lace, would give
their lives to spill
        some venom. *forecast like a damn guillotine*

I heard the man mutter.
        clouds growing fat, wind whistling
like a blade grinding for a neck

        to kiss. the calm that leads
the storm, you know well. you've received
        the finest treatment that infamy

can offer, felt the West Coast
        simmer before your insides screamed.
when you clicked your heels

        on sterile linoleum, you molted
skin, fistfuls of Ativan, & the Suboxone
        you tucked in your cheek then spit

into bathroom sinks when the nurse's
        footfalls were faint, a cure worse
than the disease. the music of your leaving

        split the dawn like a scorned lover's
daisy, the bleary Eastern coastline your new
        bedroom view. how did you end up

in this moaning city? Jackie McLean blows
        from the hi-fi's dizzy spin, quickening

your pulse as the ocean cradles the sun.

        you draw the jack of hearts & Lord
knows there's never been enough men to fill
        that open gash in your chest

& still you've refused to harden, backflipped
        belly exposed, a lone pawn
courting tenderness, the branding

        of a bruise. but resilience
be damned, winter arrives silent as a silo.
        snow will fall with an intimacy

near violent. these bones don't
        warm like they used to.
you're starved for more than blood.

        we've stashed enough honey
yet the hymns you hum rasp then
        crack through your throat.

you haven't spoken to anyone,
        not even me, in days
but when I board up the windows

        survival becomes a game
played in pairs. *we're outta smokes*
        what time you say the corner shop closed?

step four

fragments from Amy Winehouse's stepwork journal

through an act of magic i've learned how our makers dress their egos as morals & get written into scripts as strength earned up above. let me see if i can remember the trick. an animal surrounded by glass: pick one: nurture it: chase it. the glass goes black: pick one: it runs: it screams. the glass breaks: a cloud of smoke appears. when it clears: the animal is you: a flame snatched from the tip of a match to light your last sunset. you'll lose your mind over that one, can't even see you've been cheated. i've watched it a million times & i'm always as dry-eyed as the first. the beast in me has bitter taste to burn, gets off on love born to fail. when the chips start to stack above her she grips every ache in her bag big or small like the odds are all she has stands six foot six out of her heels, calls me *fucking liar* when i point out the star that will take us home. trust me—she'll kick down doors in a hurricane, let in more than the rain God sent. drowned dripping hearts down her sleeve & won't leave until you learn what *flood* means.

relapse dream

i'm dripping cherries onto the carpet & for a minute i'm jealous of my own knuckles & before i know it there's mounds of stale cake flattening into floorboards & bees fill the room & i tell myself i'm at peace with this offering at least there's cake & no one has to wait until i'm done crying to eat it & then the bees fill my mouth & my tongue fattens like it's got someplace to be & there goes eating cake & how are these sacrificial insects supposed to store honey for the winter & won't the hive miss them & won't i miss them & when i open my mouth their wings are beautiful dressed with oils & blisters & my lips swell with the sliver of another dying thing & i begin to consider the instinct required to accept your undoing no matter how fatal this staying might be & where do i even get the gall to welcome the kind of violence that greeted greater men just once before they woke up as ghosts & when will i understand the zinnias as merely a peace offering from a less forgiving god & don't they rely on the same ecosystem as the bees & don't i rely on the same ecosystem as the bees & don't i see the lesson here & how many men need to sigh *boy, them wings ain't meant to last* before i fold up my prayers & tuck them in my cheek & when will i be emptied by what a night doesn't promise instead of what it does & when will these wings unfurl however brief & prove that my shoulders are built for more than breaking falls & if all the cake is gone i said *help yourselves* at least there's blooms of honey right here in my mouth & how many bees need to die

moral inventory

          when i'm told people have more sex after funerals
than weddings, i believe it. i prefer
  to be eye-level with any creature craving
    release. when an animal evolves
to evade its predators, the predators evolve
too. baring all 32 teeth
  will not make this less violent. or will it?
    i don't know the answer—i'm really asking.
sleeping antbirds that offer their tears
to thirsty moths, the wolf that chews off
  its paw to leave the trap behind. what i saw
    as malice was, in reality, a kind of patience:
this too. a celebration of life. fur bristles
in the psalm of the moon, the gleam of a blade
  only as bright as the bulb above it.
    if you listen close you can hear prayer
in the parable of Nina Simone
bringing Angela Davis a balloon
  while she was imprisoned,
    how Angela let the latex kiss
the ceiling for weeks, heard music
in the oxygen's escape, in hands that tick
  in a city deserted. there's so much to offer
    the earth. who among us would recognize
the dead if we saw them? i've searched
my own backyard & come up with little more
  than worms. the shell in the grass
    does not match the bullet
fished from a doe's hide. still, how regal the crown
mounted in the study
  while deer struck in the road
    lay out there for months.

ode to the seagull with what looks like a chicken bone in its beak but could be another seagull's leg for all i know

i too know what it is to cannibalize
        those bent on leaving the flock,
to scavenge what's been left
        behind: the bowed limbs

of a beloved, burnt & twisted
        spoons unrecognizable
from the dining set, the break of dawn
        behind the clouds

like a killer through the curtains. once, i killed
        a cockroach & scrubbed the remains
from the floor, tile & grout carving little crosses
        into my knees, having read that a pregnant female

will release an army of eggs to replace the dead.
        a spider will spin endless hours of silk only to gorge
on a fly that missed its web & bless the broken
        flesh anyway. sometimes i wish i believed

in God just so i could summon this hunger by a name
        as noble as *feast* or *miracle*. instead i call it *luck*,
take out an insurance policy that won't
        even cover the roses

on my casket. *any port in a storm*, my grandmother
        used to say. i've choked back bile at her table
on easter sunday as the risen glowed
        all around me, not one halo in the air.

last night, the only visible body in the sky
           was mars—the infrared dot of a trained assassin
or an eye soft as prayer? all that's left
           to kill is time.

the sand surrenders to the ocean & farther out
           the ocean surrenders to the horizon.
i'm resigned to these laws of gravity
           but why don't you fly away?

on her first tour sober Amy Winehouse plays nothing but ballads & refuses to sing anything in past tense

ash-bitten by heatstroke
under house lights you move
through hallways backstage
pray to the dressing room mirror
record the defects in double columns
this all felt like instinct
while kissing a microphone
now you only lick notes
about the gap in your grin your face
bleeding out into an untethered moon

you part your lips split
like train tracks & almost expect to find
loose tendons stuck between your teeth
embarrassed by the intimacy you resist
recognition of your body
as a thing that can weep or combust
or decompose
there's peril in picking up the shards
scars like knitted seams on your hands
they are not beautiful
so you count them like hail marys
isn't this something like inventory?

a maimed mourning dove you are
attuned to the prelude of storms
pulling down windows the darkness
blooms a reflection you can't shake
you'd rather inhale the smoke
lingering like a presence
than whatever the clouds
that follow you have in store

you can still hear the applause
a chorus of insects trying to fuck
before they die
there will be no encore

step five

fragments from Amy Winehouse's stepwork journal

soaking my feet at the end of the day, i try to place all the bird calls by name. the same songs falling over themselves to reach a lover who knows how stubborn a sky can get. i give up too damn easy. if they're outside they're a hundred miles away. don't they know the sky only reflects the lost & parallel slick or lucky enough to outrun her? or that those left behind are pulled up legs first into black clouds & caned until they make rain? the tub with an endless drip i stuck out back catches every last teardrop torn or pressed & around the way the river's turned red. i wish someone had told me that recognition could be this lonely. showed up at the big house today & punched every buzzer straight down, eyes like they'd been clubbed shut & a kind of hope that can't be undone. like history a song must repeat to be a song it must repeat to be a song i hit His number til my hands hurt.

taste of cherries

sometimes we part with pain   unpronounceable
        sometimes my mother wouldn't speak

for days   sometimes we are mean & strong
        like liquor   sometimes we are soft   a *sorry* could break us

like rain   today i choose soft   i am trying to
        have a picnic under this cherry tree   eating fresh-picked

cherries peak season   such deep red   i wish
        i had someone to share them with   my neighbor

asks for a light & introduces himself   what dumb
        luck   his name is Mike   a hard tea dangles

from his mitt   an actual mitt   he is
        shoveling snow   i feel wild an almost cruel

tenderness for Mike   i imagine Mike offering me
        some of his tea   before i imagine my polite protest

i'd take a drink from someone i don't know before someone i do
        what a clever clever revealing   of my stumbledrunk past

then the comeuppance what a shame   no one
        else hears this   Pulitzer-worthy quip   hey i'm enough!

is it enough   when i die my gravestone will read
        when he walked into a room, he did not light it up

it's been 35 years & the most romantic thing
        i've been called is reckless   is that the best i can do

how dare me   so much work ahead
         i'll save it for a rainy day   right now i'm having a picnic

& listen the tree is lovely but it's blocking my view
         it's got to go   hang on   do you hear that   that voice

there's another side of the tree   *where is it*   *close one eye*
         coming from   *would you really give up all these cherries?*

i can think of a dozen different ways to break that Motown 12"
& none of them will sound as sweet as "Dancing in the Streets"

an *epidemic* they call it   lawns manicured
        like filed teeth   houses inhale
from nights without sirens   in projects

                                            who do you

        tongues swell   trunks rattle   blunt trauma
or *bad decision*   earn family time over phone lines
        or beloved's eyes   like dreary days

                                            think you're

dulled by glass thick enough   to kill an elephant
        thumb-size envelopes   wax paper printed
with a skull or an exclamation point

                                            raisin' your

        selling heaven or   something
just like it before the means to an end
        became simply   the means   our thrones

                                            voice at—

were stoops set up kingly   boomboxes
        blaring motown   *belly-rubbing music*
the oldheads called it smiles so big   our teeth

                                            who do you

        would blind you   but thrones get careworn too
spotless timbs navigate cracks   on the road
        to damascus   no one comes to fix

                                            think you—

what's broken   round here we cross
        the river   roses in our muzzles hands
fingering change in our too-

                                          who the fuck

        big pockets   scarecrows in dry season   we are
wild-eyed   displaced   *ain't afraid of nothin'*
        'cept a lighted match   these streets have

                                          do you think

fissures you can't see   veins that
       stay hidden   with blindfolds tied we walk
a razored line between heaven

                                                                                          you are—
       & here   the climb uphill has filled our mouths
with last year's harvest   slowed us to crawl   we sharpen
       our *please* & *thank you*

                                                                                         lock that door
freeze like bedroom drafts
       open wide   to free our pleading   but instead exhale
a yawn   a slate gray sky   an arm gone limp
                                                                                           behind you.

moral inventory

it's june   i wouldn't know
        but for the robins   singing

their robinsongs   i can't imagine
        what they're on about   i'm bored

with my own slow dying i lick   the spoon
        sticky with curdled cream my beloved's fingertips   the pages stuck

then smeared   i can't remember the moment i wanted to stop
        doing bad things   when i understood

certain kinds of ruin   can be useful   the candle i light
        then snuff out

O demiurge   i'm too tired   to talk
        to you   with prayers like spent shells i haven't swept

the stoop all month   even the sky   dying such a beautiful backdrop
        for our all the time dying

grief

how do i make room
for all this grief?
what wells are deep
enough? or is it grief
that needs to
make room for me?
is there enough space
inside
the damp
sprawling mouth of grief?
between its peeling
lips, pockets
to fall into? *make room*
i hear
though i'm not
quite sure
where it's coming from
make room.

is my grief as grievous
as other griefs?
if i wrap my grief
in sleek looping
ribbons will it be
as beautiful
as your grief? or is it
grief that grants us
our beauty? will my birthmarks
& scars be beautiful too?
my simpering, my sniveling
at the awe
-stirring sight
of the dogwoods
in full regalia?

to what else will
grief—indiscriminate
& gawking—give
its beauty? the glinting talons
of a hawk, the slick fist
that withdraws
when i'm famished?

did grief sell me
a dream? hand me
the keys? take me
on a test drive
through the dirty dusk?
when did this
shady play
for my pockets
go down? was i too busy
trying to pick the moon
rusted penny of the sky
from the lip of the ocean
to notice? it often distracts me
the moon, i mean. i apologize
to my grief. my grief
whispers salaciously
its tongue gummy
with the scent of honey
-comb, balmy breath
dissolving
in my ear—*it's going to be
a good summer. just wait
til you see how this baby tears.*

& tear, it does: up
& down
the molten asphalt—the smell
of singed hair steeped
in my nostrils, nauseating.

that is grief. every notebook
i ever spilled
myself into, every checkbook
i ever peeled
myself out of—torn up
by grief. my cheeks hot
with heartache—that
too is grief.
grief holds my head
under
-water, little bubbles
swimming
to the surface, tiny
round miracles
inside them, grief.
artful grief. conniving
grief. sniff-out-the-jewels-
in-a-room-full-of-thieves
grief. need-bigger-arms-
to-carry-all-this grief.
my grief eats an entire season's
worth of strawberries
in one fell swoop, spits blood
at the camera lens, dances
on graves. my grief has muscles
that ripple in the sun.
my grief is boundless
infinite. my grief is always
one step
ahead of me.

i'm tired.

when i'm just about ready to surrender
to my grief, my grief softens
& shakes, eases its grip, gently releases
its hand from the nape of my neck.

the gasp that flows, my lungs freshly
freed once i drink the sharp salty
air—that's gratitude—it's mawkish i know—
stretching & yawning
across an unreachable summer sky.

so many miles just to slip this skin.

step six

fragments from Amy Winehouse's stepwork journal

everyone is busy dreaming in this house on fire. thirty stories high & no telling how many friends are inside gambling away the only stars still crazy enough to shine. a bar fight against the bar just to chase a failing flame. i snatch a bottle off the curb & let it fly my eyes following its flight as it lands a hair's width from a bird. i'd separate what's left of myself from the ground if i could stomach the height. or the comedown. truthfully these tears probably started falling weeks ago but i tell myself it must be the smoke in my eyes, puff on a Marlboro & watch the house light up the night. i'd give anything or just everything for a new ache. my heart sticks to my guts like chipped glass, which is i guess a way of saying it's broken, but what a tired thing to call holding the past like a lover. what a bitter reminder that the same slick matter in my chest that pumps blood & keeps me breathing makes me kiss the river until all you can see are my legs lonely & strong not even fighting.

DMX teaches me how to pray

there are creatures in the wild who, through fast
        or famine, refuse to lick even their own wounds.
once, i followed a pack of dogs until one peeled off

        to bless miles of snow with blood
before crawling into the private mouth
        of a cave. i waited a week until it reemerged,

fur fully translucent, like spidersilk dowsed
        in a slat of dawn. its teeth were so clean
i gripped its jaws steady & stood before the reflection

        to watch my pulse beat backwards.
you can't blame me for tearing down even the dark
        stars on the long walk home. it's cold

living with ghosts. one way to get close to God
        is to sin as hard as you can.
like a spent bullet pulled from a brick wall i confessed

        to crevices & cracked ceilings until i discovered
"Ready to Meet Him" by DMX like a scripture.
        X taught me the voice of atonement

& my own were one & the same: the ricochet
        of his barely tweaked call & response, arms
raised gently on the cover to meet the camera

        in a bath of blood. i haven't raised my lips outside
sacrilege since. if we found eternity, would we even know
        what to do with it? God doesn't

reward good intention any more than he grants mercy
        for its scarcity but pokes us while we sleep
like dry ice charring a corpse. once, i hid from a storm

        in a manger surrounded by bales of hay
ruined by rain. the horses bucked with hunger
        while i lay lit up like a lemon grove

with a stray straw clamped in my teeth.
        beyond the pasture of downed trees, split
or bent like knees, i caught the horizon blink

        then spent the next seven years
trying to find where it ends. i hate
        how obvious i'd become—oblivious

most people don't care. i learned a shadow's
        length becomes grace we can summon
with the flick of a wrist: the crack in a doorway

        lonely in the dark. a roman candle
crying in the mouth of a crypt. i see now
        that X found repentance across fields

tangled in gauze, shepherding his dogs
        like a rosary passing parted lips.
between the bark & balm of bluster

        he sang a hymn so tender we forgot
what we were mourning, aching toward
        the moon so low it polished the snow.

*aubade with Nina Simone who sang "Sinnerman"
& the whole world lost its balance*

10 Amendments help guide you
when your life has been spared.

the same number of Commandments.

rounded & firm. a peddling tool.

still, I find the calming utility of counting
useful.

my footfalls on a staircase

one
two
three

four
five
six cracks in a sidewalk, a clock's fixed
click

at dawn

one
two
three
four...

▽

I once heard a Chinese proverb that teaches
after you save a person's life, you assume
eternal responsibility—a burial plot scooped

fresh, clean & waiting, will continue to linger
beautifully. red sea urchins live to be over two
hundred years old. cats have nine

lives. fallible beings that we are, but one.
when blessed with your own ephemeral
body, will you wet your lips with gratitude

or guilt, heavy as cast iron? once you arrive
at renascence, learn to savor the little things:
a dollop of light dipping through

the curtain. it takes eight
minutes & twenty
seconds for the sun to meld
a glint into our living blue.

▽

in moments of desperation, hands will be drawn to clasp. prayer is a kind of instinct, devotion a steady throb. in 1965, a repentance groaned for every minute that Nina Simone purged a room, rapt. she needed nothing more than a tittering rhythm to bring her own hands together, soldered tools of God. gingerly snapped fingers find cadence & the Earth in its mournful way begins to unravel its dead skin. the arithmetic of dry timber & a stray spark.

▽

it takes 782 blueberries to fill a bucket & only one blackberry for your tongue to unfold the shade of a gut shot.

▽

a bullet's precise exit

        —solitary.

the cold, impersonal touch
of a doctor

        —five fingertips.

the soft-focus glow of a dream
like a yellowed ring

around a drain

        —fourteen spokes.

where it gurgles & gasps:

        escape route.

▽

the mist of a mid-autumn morning
paws at my skin. I lean
into its petrichor, drink
the milky balm,
begin my ascent:

one

        two

                three

I stop counting when I spot the craquelure, a heaven

                that hangs

                        the dirty sky.

        ▽

nature retreat nocturne with Amy Winehouse

    in an american movie   this is where you would sigh
say *look at this view*   but you're not looking
at the mountains   you're examining the lines
on your palms   the blemish gazing back
in a compact mirror   as the sun swims
        in another dying sky
but you're not looking at the sunset   you're thinking
about the tip you left the waiter at lunch   surely
you could afford to leave more by now   you're not
looking at the lake
        its idyllic calm
you're playing with the flesh on your thighs firm
as dragonfruit   you've been eating   so well
everyone has admired your healthy glow   a new dime's
shine   you look up & the night
        is laced
with the best broken china &   you   are the note
that peels off   from a song & joins   the crimson
constellation
        who said God
doesn't give with both hands   a heaven in these clouds
close enough to choke on   the distance inviting
as an open throat   in the american movie
this is where you would stretch your arms   throw back
your head   say *all this is mine*   but you blink slowly
        say *all this will be gone soon*
it's getting so late it's early   you're traipsing down the trail
back to the warmth & musk   of other lives   dawn pulses
black & blue   a dog barks   a bell rings   you're forgetting something

step seven

fragments from Amy Winehouse's stepwork journal

as holy as the moon hung close i cried for no relief i couldn't recite by heart, stupid & fearless inside a night so black it was almost blue. cherries lonely as an alibi grow red as Mars where the sun won't bleed. some light takes years to reach us but like a headless bird flying in a free fall the stars could already be dead. dreams of war & a flood no one gets saved from keep my head on the ground listening for the fire that screams underneath & watching for foot tracks that don't get lost in the rain, eyes hardened & endless as God's silence. i've spent a lifetime in the throes of Heaven looking for a sky mad enough to save me.

on why Miles Davis quit playing ballads

> You know why I quit playing ballads?
> Because I love playing ballads.
> MILES DAVIS

once a woman who claimed
she loved me carried me

down half a Brooklyn block
on the hood of her car

then spat me onto blacktop
like she'd forgotten

her manners. in her rearview
mirror my eye's corner

caught her cold reflection
dark eyes & skin of a crone

rippling like a dried fig.
i imagine she managed

to muffle a curse, skid a puff
of smoke but didn't bother

to glimpse how much of me
she'd left behind. don't look

at me like that. i was there
hapless as flesh crumpled

in a canon. consider the shape
i take when i hover, all right

angles, hands loosening like tea
leaves. now consider a woman

in Coney Island, a makeshift
orchestra's pit on a bench nearby

bending her limbs into halos
a minuet she's learned to dance

alone, marking time & loss
on swollen wood. the tune lilts

as her head swivels, curls cloaked
in a leopard's splotched print

the lonely predator
stalking prey in solitude

as the sky's glare softens
to a glow. i turn my attention

to the laughing gulls gliding
over tenements where mud

-caked boots grace every
welcome mat & children shot

-gun clouds with tongues rolled
like holy scripts. listen carefully.

the dancing maiden's cackle
cracks like kindling & somewhere

close by figs snap the wings off
wasps & swallow them whole.

she leaves a box near brimming
to rot but on return will find them

merely ripened. i don't know
how else to tell you this

but no one is coming to save you.

the buck moon is full & wild
-fire red at our windows

smoke crawling from rubble
across the barren heart

-land to creep into our bedrooms
trailing blood. instead of crying

wolf, i went looking for them
scurrying after paw prints

the shape of plums, plumes
dancing around their jaws.

in this way, my body becomes
communion. in this way

i am not eaten but savored.

as the car peeled off
i coughed up a feather

blinked at a doorway
a woman her eyes wide

with a mother's tender
gloom on her stoop

loomed like a fig tree
above its fallen fruit

folded her arms over
sirens she sighed

honey, you need to love yourself more

& like the moon bleary
through a whorl of ash

i saw my static heart, still
beating.

dirge for the last night of Eric Dolphy's life, part II

in Berlin, *shock* becomes a word without rendering. a horn is muted, lights the warm hue of bourbon. it sits there dumbly: one brass syllable twisted into entropy. a holy messenger slips between fissures like sharp wind through an open mouth. in its raw pink the vulture's slow spiral around heaven's floor. even in this dying a drop of blood drains like the glow from dead stars. but history isn't kind to men who play God, damn near lethal, infected with *d'evils*. & just like that, a body is freed of its haunting. a transatlantic song unfurls missed notes & pitches pried from rigor mortis. even the gods starve.

all my attempts at meditation end in shouting matches with ghosts

& when her cab eased down myrtle avenue / well that was likely the last i'll ever see of her / i did not watch / her slushy ebb i was distracted by the sky / dirty as the bottom of an ashtray / now i know someone out there must be thinking / *how prosaic* but this is merely heartbreak / the sky is the sky / it's unlanguageable / even planes get lost in its latent prose / even this temperature-bending grief stumbles / under its piles of soot i see a man below a pale halo / wearing a coat like a flag whipping away its filth / hauling trophies two arms full / to a trash heap & i know what it is to crave / freedom from victory / to pray off the gilt & glitter it guts out of you / maybe the trophies aren't his spoils but scars that burn / smokeless like psalms or votives / closer to skin than salt / maybe he's vain or he's proud / they cheapen what's made for bleeding / maybe they don't belong to him at all / but a beloved who left them to languish / until he could no longer take it / he simply does not need the reminders / the gimcrack gold's every curve seared to memory / the sharp glint keeps him from sleep / he wants release / i envy this man / to walk away in repose so cavalier he appears to hover / to hunger / for absence like the magician / who rips the sheet from beneath the wine & candles losing / none of his sacrament / not a drop / not a flicker / tongue fixed as spots on a leopard

last night i turned off the pilot light

certain the heat from my cheeks
could dredge up any wayward

set of wings. it wasn't until i ran
out of room on my forearms

that i learned the difference between
picking scabs & the stretch of skin

that smooths over—the way wind whips sand
into glossolalia. i find a branch that won't

flood my throat with pine oil when i snap it
whisper *i'm sorry*, use it to draw a tidy line

then tiptoe directly across. God catches me
by the ponytail, a creature worth saving

but when i spit up the Eucharist, i don't know
how to tell Him it isn't because i'm not hungry

i just can't stop laughing. *must be nice*, He scoffs,
to be so sated. the word *sated* is sharp as a shark's

sense for blood. my toothiness is getting on
God's nerves. i've been learning to breathe

so quiet the thrum of a lightbulb is like thunder
inside a magpie. last night when i kissed halos

into midnight i swear i felt Mary's hem skimming
my fringe & stowed my breath in a jar for sins

still simmering, placed it open on the windowsill.

step eight

fragments from Amy Winehouse's stepwork journal

to make hurt real a song's gotta be written like a set of rules: sniff out what's been dying in the walls, start a fire high enough to burn planes out of the sky. all i can remember is how tired it all felt the last time you kicked in my door—how i'd probably forget it by morning the way i'd wake up forgetting the stars. or that guitar i played too hard. the new Badu i didn't play enough. the weed i stole, wearing a Beasties tee i didn't buy. the Moschino bra underneath, battered pumps & Gucci bag i can't find. Jamaica & Spain, i slept through. Miami moon i cried under. the airport where i punched that rich boy outside the mile high club. his wife too screaming like she was born to sing backup for men who have bedrooms for eyes. what did i leave out? the boxes out back spilling what was left of my life? the curb in the rain i called home for a night? what then? my *heart*?

arguing with my sponsor's ghost about the last place i saw him alive

i'm not thinking about you when i veer left
onto Flatbush Avenue. something's off

in the traffic's gleam—high beams
framing last rites & new frontiers.

God caught more hands than hymns
can crack last time he came down here

slumming, shooting dirty pool
for pocket change with guttersnipes

through the Second Coming.
the call to repent has been crystal:

wait patiently until permitted to leave
or you're led out by your chain.

but i'm fed three times a day here, can't say
i go hungry anymore. i even had that dream

about the future again, the one where
i'm the last cellist alive lost in a minuet

atop a lake of thawing ice. you weren't in it.
now i stare down strangers on the F train

faces pinched & longer than a wet weekend
imagine they've been fantasizing every fissure.

at a bodega, Ms. Bonnie Raitt is sighing somewhere
overhead. she can't make her heart feel something

it don't. when i pass the used car lot, stars light up
the frost on all the domestics, discounted

& longing for deliverance. it was here i loved you
a bend in the road sharp & desperate as prayer.

the night of Dexter Gordon's comeback

we consider our reckoning across aisles dank & narrow

with palms so soft they could cradle
a cracked egg. in the ashen end-
of-day, we recommit

to crimes of passion, raise sacrifices

out of cinders like chalices to our lips. by morning
the cruel workmanship of a bee
brings the colors in every flower

to pop: pink trim of primrose, purple sweep of hyacinth, probing

red of peony. smeared fingers that crave the cleanse
of an open throat: plush & carnivorous, their beauty
unblinking.

I just walked into the room & they applauded.

then cherries, so many cherries, the first of springtime. in their pluck
is a hint of ignominy: in their glint, a sliver
of psalm. we shield our eyes & the marrow in our bones

vibrates. how sweet the sound. how sweet—

that winter i wrote the same poem over & over

since childhood i've been consumed
by maps
    moonstruck by miles
covered while motionless
        as a carcass
in the back cab of the truck
my grandfather used
to haul whatever it was he used to haul
i'd pore over
    the crinkled routes he'd take all
across the eastern seaboard
even now when blessing
      a land new
-to-me with gloom
      i stand before
placards charting
public transportation & courses
for wandering
    wobblelimbed
up & down the webbed
      streets infinite
tracks trace the arc of any heart
ache
 sunstrobed or rainswept i'll spend
hours bewitched
    by the crescent path from
montparnasse to père lachaise
in paris or the cobble-stoned
      back alleys
that twist through the alfama district
in lisbon
  like damp hair wrapped
around a finger or the bending

                        cartilage when it
breaks
don't get me started
on miniature city models
                    a crisis brimming
a craving really
            to crush the whole damn thing
one swift movement my foot makes
its sole a culprit
        caked with debris
guilty too my admittedly blasé
heart not off my sleeve
                as the poets love
to say but a wet rose in my teeth

years ago i worked
at a bar a night like any night
                crawled forward
a woman beckoned me
            asked *are you playing this*
to chase us out?
      (i was) *because as long as you play*
leonard cohen i'm not going anywhere
                  i could see
the sum of our affair
already stretching like molasses across
the sky to be read in stars
              so caustic & close
i didn't know
      if they'd burn or crown us
she stayed til 4am & then the next
two years
      without ever really
falling in love

upon hearing Prince sing "Purple Rain" at First Avenue
in Minneapolis in 1983, i begin to understand my mother's love life

> *I don't want your money, no no no no*
> *I don't even think I want your love—*
>
> PRINCE ROGERS NELSON

I confess. my sorrow will eat more
of me than any kind of hunger.

I steam up phone booths with tears,
I overdress for my own funeral.

my eager heart is my mother's
eager heart.

heaven is darker than I was led to
believe, so I take light

where I can: my throat bright
with amethysts, the kitchen's dim glow

like a searchlight in a prison yard.

my mother loves most what enables her
to be lonely.

the ashtray is glutted with hours,
the car won't even start anymore,

but I know times are changing.
new wind brushes the jasmines,

their bloom leans away from me.
the moon waxes & wanes.

I hate to see anything so lovely alone.

step nine

fragments from Amy Winehouse's stepwork journal

you are the blue jay restless as a lullaby the night before Christmas blazing above miles & miles of green. i'm sorry all my urges were spent between wishes blown on silence & spilling every last drop of me until there was no blood left to spill. useless & inevitable a shot you see coming. a plague that could turn your holiest river red. how do i even begin to unlearn touch as song? my body a battle lost? i'm sorry all my spite found homes in verses, the letters best unsent or better burned. i'm all churning guts & pride, an unkept kitchen. i save my regrets for rooms relieved of light: the union between an unmade bed & my lover, breath faded freshly bludgeoned. i'm sorry i'm stubborn as a losing gambler. i never loved anyone that didn't come to me clean as stars & leave a crime.

my beloved forgets how to pray

still stretches in the morning toward nothing.
        a corner with a desk & chair, a glass

        of water reaching for its rim. repeats
the two shortest surahs in the qur'an with a whisper

that wouldn't fog a window. in arabic, there is a word
        that means both *breath* & *spirit*. ghosts dance

        around her lips like a pilot light, bidding them
to part, hypnosis coaxed with jewel-encrusted horns.

in a cellar not far from here, wine waits years to peak
        before a bottle is cracked open only to empty

        a bruise. oil leaps from the controlled heat
of cast iron & tattoos a comma onto someone's wrist.

once, i wandered into church after bringing my body
        to the brink of combustibility. i can't remember

        what the priest told me, but know the photo
taken by heart—me, pale in the pews, windless & tranquil.

now i wake everyday & try to do less
        harm than the day before. still, one doesn't choose

        their obsessions. i couldn't help myself when i stole
your wallet just to pretend i was you. don't forgive me. i don't

even know how to apologize. what's the next right thing?
        in aramaic, the words for *rope* & *camel* are one

        letter off. one of the jewel-horned ghosts urged me
to trust God but to tie my camel. i can't even trust myself.

i left the rope wriggling in the wind, tried to whip
        & gallop my way through the needle's eye

        only to end up eating sand. my beloved lives
where blasphemy & the blade race to reach an open

throat—a lamb's sacrifice & requital called a kinder
        silence swirling to meet the same drain.

        she sheathes her hair under the soft strain
of satin, her tongue cribbed so tight in her cheek

it throbs. i've staked out street corners all winter
        to draw my body's outline thick enough

        to see through the fog on rooftops.
she drew one breath & my corpse disappeared

like a kiss dissolving on a quay. here we mistake
        the hawks' restless circle for a carousel

        in the sky, car tires spit out by ocean tides
for discarded halos of sunbathing angels. you might

call these miracles or something closer to mischief
        like sirens forging stars to hoodwink cartographers.

        as far as they are, we still whisper—a song
so forlorn spirits guiding ships to wreck long for the shore.

the summer after DMX *died every rainfall felt like a benediction*

the way i'm loved in a grocery store is as good as any other.
we move at a pallbearer's pace, soak up whatever salves
the streets don't reap, collect leaking welts like pennies
from a well. i don't blame the mosquitoes. i siphon off all
my lifelines, weep like i drank all the wine. when God visits
He paints the town a darker thirst, the wells so empty they sigh.
we tell stories about the days before you knew me biblically.
the disciples washed my feet. you spoke in tongues & i refused
to believe you ever cut loose a string of syllables i wouldn't lap up
like the moon's reflection. in a painting, i point out the blunders
of the galaxy. most stars don't explode. they have their moment
then they die: the butterfly once feared now perched
on your finger. the pearl one waxwing pitches another.
the twitch that parts your lips when i tell you something true.

God loves everybody, don't remind me

a snake goes blind the last time it sheds skin, a body
refused. I've found my own senses dulled once freed of some body:

a cello's strings bending out of tune. the first time I saw a praying
mantis was in a housing project courtyard, a ballet of bodies

& the perfume of poverty. my aunt accosting me, *it's illegal to kill
them*: a mercy for predators she didn't allow her own body.

a block from here, a boy had his life snatched on the wrong side
of midnight, chalk drawn to crown his cold body

under a sign outside a sports bar: *no gang colors allowed*.
I watch from the curb, my heart an intruder in my body

bleating its dirge: the ugly work of loneliness, blood trickles,
pools in my palms. my chest caves into the shape of a body.

before my exile I sow my grief, give dead flowers back to the earth
but won't accuse God of injustice. I know He loves every body

don't remind me. stripped & nameless in the Land of Nod, my skin
as thin as an insect's wings: the only proof that I still live in this body.

withdrawal dream with Amy Winehouse chain-smoking
in the dining hall of a rehabilitation center & plotting her escape

        i know my guilt   is bred

to kill me   still   i feed it

        crickets wolf   spiders discarded   husks

          tiny wrens   from the marshlands

                                                            my palm

an open grave   no one here   knows

               my name   my face

marked   in the flicker

          of every hunter's eye   my fevers

have razed　　　　　　　this land　　　　　　　any field will burn

　　in the right climate　　　　　　　my unraveling

　　　　　　　　　　　　　　　　　　　　　　dazzling even

　　from the mountaintops　　　　i've mauled

the most churlish lions　　　　to earn　　　　these stripes

yet　　　　i wish i'd made more　　　　than

　　　　a mausoleum　　　　from this

　　　　　　　　　　　　　　　　hunger

i've seen children　　　　curse the sky　　　　men turn

　　to open wounds　　　　　　for warmth

                    they loved me   harsh

like northern ice   i loved

                them soft   like island moss

                    love has never been   much different

                                                           from thirst

    if you listen   close enough

         you can   hear   my skin

                                                    crawl

step ten

fragments from Amy Winehouse's stepwork journal

okay i'll just say it: i cheated. you were on the list. you were the list. i searched under every rock, tore up all the carpets for a new place to hide you—your Diesel jeans, smoking pipe, the will i wrote & left on your desk entrusting you with only the rain. now blue light peeks from behind the door & i try to shove the jeans under the frame to stop the crime it makes my kindness but they just go up in flames. i tread the room, now on fire a fuckery of Freudian fates. shadows mule lovers' skulls like debts of war, my heart an empty purse. wait. there's a penny from the year you were born. is that enough?

i am having so much fun without you

the sun is a natural thespian
has presence, inspires

prayer, commands
maybe more

than its fair share
of the stage

all elbows.

we gape, wince
celebrate

when the moon
blots it out like a black eye.

i'm told Love can take you
to another planet

sometimes it leaves you there.

before she learned the most
dramatic use

of the front door
my beloved taught me how

to slice a mango
a fruit she can't go home

& eat in Cairo, the knife
blushing

from her touch, her hands

nimble, innate
as if she were dismantling

the rainbowed
guts of a bomb.

i still peel the skin with my fingers

sink teeth into flesh
that clings—

sneakers dangling
above the street.

my neighbor keeps a funeral placard
on his dashboard

even after weeks of sunlight
have gifted the glum message

a magic hour glow.

his tires hug each curve
in the blacktop

like a tick crawling up a swan's neck.

blunt smoke carries a chorus
through the cracked car windows—

we're on our way to a lovely wreck, lovely wreck
la dee da dum, la dee da dum
the trapeze artist breaks her neck, breaks her neck
la dee da dum, la dee da dum—

look closer

the sun is only a desperate star

disheveled
like it just sauntered off

a belle & sebastian album cover.

its light kisses the sidewalk
the sidewalk skins my palm.

brick walls borrow my blasphemy
bounce it back

limber, lingering
a bit of reverb.

*on Whitney Houston's acceptance speech at the 2001 BET Awards
& why i pray in the dark*

the song begins not where prayer
escapes daylight or sweat hits
even the mezzanine but above you

like angels who don't love you.
when your own hands prove

sleight you bite your fist
& turn blasphemous toward
the sky but there are two ways

to dull your fangs: rust or strike
bone. no one told you that
you couldn't do both.

like an emerald encrusted
on a bayonet sometimes
you find yourself luminous

& near dying. you ask sorrow
to lose your number, wear black
to the intervention, spawn rivals

in every ghost town
with barstools still swerving.
it never hurts to praise

the salvaged limbs you had
to use to build your ladder.

white lights unfurl & follow
you, practically devotional
from the rafters where saints

keen & stalk the dark they feed on.
what some called delirium
you called sunset. beauty will be

something you can kill or not
be at all. everything you've sung
about baptism feels more
like drowning.

i admit it i've never seen a falling star

that isn't a metaphor. i miss each flicker the way i skirt a train
        just in time to pillage what's left behind: crushed coins
tucked for luck, to flip or plink a tip. whether wishes squeezed
        from copper or blunders looped in home movies, my highs
are contagious as bee stings so i catch what i can keep.
        if Ganymede's story is one of divinity, i am Dionysus fresh
out of rehab—worshippers bent before me with robes reduced to rags,
        my thyrsus strewn in some storm drain i can't reach, honey
crystallized white as a bone wrapped in wilted ivy. Ganny is well-versed
        in refusal with a wink, snickering while i fail to snatch
my lonely wand among the grate's graveyard growing vines & rust.
        is there a wrong way to pronounce *mock
tail*? Ganny seems to relish sketching stories with scorn
        each time i try to order. when there are no gods left
to serve, i will serve myself. once, i loved a woman whose crown
        now floods the night sky, or so i'm told. i've been searching for her
ring of stars to light my way home since my chalice turned green
        but i'm stuck still on barstools, kneeling in back alleys
where i tempt myself with even the dust motes that refuse to land.
        i've granted hands that gave gold to everything
in reach, but what's the use in any trove when a lover's mercy
        glitters but won't glow? hell, even immortality
has its limits. born cutting my own teeth on curbs, i've never seen
        heads actually roll so i flip the severed crown
flattened in my pocket quick to kiss
        my palm before it bounces through the rusted grate
where a glint simmers & i squint to glimpse
        a dim spark. a scorched stone. a dying star.

unholy

this poem is unholy scarcely a drop
of suffering to be found. angels protest

terrified don't fly
but dive through clouds of smoke

trying to occupy space. i am
graceless caught

like a spiderweb in your lashes.
when you break my fall

you are calm as a fruit stand in new york
& maybe as strange. the gunslinger

effect deduces that in a duel
the shooter who draws first

will lose so i'm careful

what i'm good at.
i was born gripping pearl

handles piercing mirrors
like a cardinal breaking glass

upon seeing its reflection.

once i saw you & didn't blink
until the sky bled daylight

lips slick with expired moon.
i've shed slabs of flesh

like spent shells from lonely snipers
who graze azaleas to spare their targets

but i would savor even the skin
you pluck from your teeth.

when a sunflower is full of seeds
it will bend its head

to cut the long trip
home. this seems almost joyful

letting go like the dead
butterfly you preserved

in a plastic sleeve only to dream
a gale of wings ringing you

a halo. vigilant as a finch
in a snowstorm you filch

the dark focus from magic hour
reduce the sun to a flickering

votive kissing your shoulder.

if you move
even a little i will inhale

the tender planet of your head
tuck its damp mess

beneath my tongue
& scatter your curls

like buckshot across the night sky.

delays & departures in an airport bar with Amy Winehouse

but first the question of the guillotine   how heartbreak
can turn you heel   before any judge
or jury   she shivers so hard the pinup on her bicep
appears to sing   sullen & operatic   a kind of warble
i haven't heard   since a woman   like a storm
cleaned out every corner of my own heart

you can't rival the dead for love

everywhere blades   the lime wheel on an untouched
glass of seltzer   a wish like a razor whistling
under-tongue   she winces   the sting of citrus
kissing broken skin   *imagine gettin' what we ask for?*
points out the bruises on our knees   ripe plums
the coins gleaming from a nearby fountain
a bed of severed crowns crawling   up the wall
have better luck spittin' up dice

you can't rival the dead for love

the departure board blinks   a sandstorm rages
in her glass   bubbles whorling   wisps of smoke
need to use the loo right-quick   her heels click   outside
a night so pure the trees preen   i catch the glow the moon
shucked off   a scythe in the sky   our plane a silhouette
dancing   across its face

you can't rival the dead for love

step eleven

fragments from Amy Winehouse's stepwork journal

kitchen clean as a licked whisk. empty bottles long gone, wrapped up & sent off in black bags. outside the birds feel closer than ever flying around a foot track's dead-end where something i can't see but know is still alive won't give up. i light a match, relieve the blue flame of the moon's shadow. as it dances through the room, my lips as still as blood run cold—but still but still—how can i swear to God if singing, if even singing…listen i promise. after i sleep—deep & heavy as the world's last plague—i'll find the will. Your will. clinging inside like a baby in a well. sing me home.

slow singing & flower bringing

this is another poem about birds, maybe even an ode
to the ravens thought to expel their young from the nest.

their first lesson to fend for themselves, to grow
or die. now in collectives swathing the sky we call them

an *unkindness*. in grade school we learn on multi-colored
construction paper that a heart symbolizes love & only later

does science nullify our naiveté, teach us its shape
does not curve into perfect arcs but resembles something

akin to a beating fist. we offer them palms skyward
toward those who tuck another slur under

tongue. history has been known to canonize
its blunders. my mother expected a girl

but there was a storm, my first curl
licked by rain. every night she left

feed on our windowsill for a wounded raven
no matter how many scars dressed her skin.

in this poem I cannot tell a grackle from a blackbird
only tropes like wings that don't beat. broken wings

if you will. these ravens do not sing into daybreak
with a melody bruised & beautiful but rather dirges

dark as coal mines. this one raven, a penumbra
flared with horror & midnight around the eyes—

please let me be clear: this is not a ghost
story. everyone in this poem is very much alive

like coffins just the same. how many tin cans my mother
left on our cracked stoop to nourish the hobbled bird

I've exhausted limbs keeping track. in the wild
the weak are often picked off by predators

but there's a kindness in this culling.
put it this way: prey sense hunger

before their hunters. I've found myself
gun-shy while windows flashed with skies

protesting dusk & before I knew it the glint of wet silk
strewn across dry linen, bedrooms pooled with feathers

flesh opened, blood stirring—a feeding frenzy.
it's never long before scarcity begets cannibalism

where scarlet blooms in even the kindest nights.
the moon in its socket blinked

an ill omen. I didn't listen. ill as in flightless:
ill as in heartsick. I was wrong too. this is a ghost story.

The Truth

I said I wouldn't mention *death* in this poem.[1]

I said I wouldn't mention the creek.[2]

I said I wouldn't mention the only photo I have of us.[3]

I said I wouldn't mention Klonopin in the bathroom sink.[4]

I said I wouldn't mention the phone call, or any phone calls.[5]

I said I wouldn't mention the music.[6]

I said I wouldn't mention anything so prosaic as parking lots cracked or hearts.[7]

I said I wouldn't mention mothers.[8]

I said I wouldn't mention body in the creek.[9]

& now you expect, what? for me to talk about train tickets, tape torn to salvage them, fruit left to rot?[10]

---

1 I respectfully request a grace period.
2 If it were the ocean, would it matter?
3 A messy bedroom on the bottom lip of Philadelphia.
4 Dead insects: Debris: Driftwood.
5 Static clinging to my ear.
6 "Hand of Doom" by Black Sabbath ouroboros.
7 How we unknotted them & smiled.
8 Scorned daughters.
9 I haven't. I wouldn't.
10 This reference is a broken link. Please contact your administrator.

the profits of gravity

the french don't say *i miss you*.
they say *tu me manques*—

you are missing from me.
isn't that lovely?

i've severed
enough flesh

i can't recognize
my reflection in storefronts—

my gasp is a shrillness
that t-pain would jump to correct.

remind me again
where the line breaks

in a sunset.

remind me again
why empires fall.

this love is so lyrical i want to break it.

two waxwings
in washington square

mingle
feed each other fresh berries

then fly off like applause.

i often wonder
if they're named after icarus

& what remains
of my merciful side slips out

*please stay close
there's so much out there*

that profits off gravity

so many dogwoods in bloom
so many pomegranates to peel.

the ocean isn't haunted it just holds our dead

i see clouds reflected in my phone, the pigeons
feeding beneath me through the slats in a bench.
a man at a power plant cuts a wire thick as a king's ring
& thousands of seabirds disappear.
i am selfish. i want all of the curses.
walking with crossed legs, my frame deflated
since you knew me, i'm often weighed down
by all this useless beauty, a lost pilgrim
who won't get off his knees.
toiling toward the ocean like a dead comet.
you don't try to leave. you do or you don't.
don't you tell me about patience. i have counted
from one to ninety between walls & their crooked
picture frames ignoring yesterday & tomorrow
with neatly sewn tulips, my knuckles hard & white
as teeth. i have walked water parted so long
i've become the shore. you were right about the end.
landfall makes no difference.
the lonely take their lightness literally, ride wind
whipped from wasps' wings past the waves
& breakers. the dead crack their collar bones
& still come up swinging.
it wasn't always this hard. it was often impossible.
a bell rings, its tongue useless
without human touch. funny, i don't remember
there being any churches around here. if you see me
with my knees bent, hands clasped too tight
to pry open, i know i look like a boxer
clinching to catch breath but i'm holding
us in place like the moon losing its last chance
to go rogue. i'm cautious but nothing is harmless.
everyday the sun is late to kiss the shore. i try to drown
the bully swan forgetting he knows how to swim.
you are here, somewhere in the wind

blowing sand on the road that won't stay behind me.
i need you to know i'm still terrified.

step twelve

fragments from Amy Winehouse's stepwork journal

I wake again from my dream, the one where my killer is filing his knife on a chair made from all my past lovers' skulls. only this time I finally remember how it ends: a nightingale snatches the knife & tears off, its shine disappearing behind the sun. I marry the bird wearing a dress closer than God's shadow our union wrapped in a cloud of smoke with no flame. back in my bed my body is bathed in a blue so brutal & beautiful I can drift down any river & reach dry land just two hands & a snap away from holy. outside the moon spills across the sky separating the dark from what's left of the night, rain returning to nature spent & soaked in the ground. once I drew floods behind every upturned ship, now every drop I ever lifted from dry spell to hurricane is burned before it hits my lips or licks my heels. all my crimes & curbside crying sworn into song. but tonight is mine. my skin is warm with stars hanging like keys, birds pouring in soft as sanctuaries. I close my eyes & part my lips not knowing what to sing but knowing it has been sung.

on Survivor's Guilt ending with "Ruff Ryders' Anthem" by DMX

i thought i saw your face, your unmistakable
gait on the 6 train
—i'm wrong.
blessings refused maybe
or imagined.
it is May. i am tired of being naive.
the day you died my life was shaved ice
& shocked mint, whiskey still cutting a hem
closer than the garment seamed by God.
maybe, dear reader, you were thirsty once
or twice upon a time. maybe we don't speak
anymore but on a day of days i sated something
in you less sin than sunder. by which i mean
these were the Springs i made of everyone
a requiem. by which i mean
my lonely was unrequited.
pewter cups clicked like prayer beads
as i crafted juleps for prim mouths
grown wild beneath wide brims while men
cinched into uniform whipped horses, drank
at the waters of Lethe
& i too am not blameless of brute
force in the service of darkening soil.
i have forgotten that old friends are dead.
my beloved wears a blue threadbare shirt
of her old school's hockey team, games
she'd attend purely to see two bodies
exchange a violence approaching love.
at what point does the body cease
its sovereignty & become a thing
to be plucked & played?
if you're lucky, it will bring you to your knees.
i walk past a movie theater,
everyone outside seems so displeased

cast in the lobby's static glow.
is it not enough to sit somewhere
dark & see a beautiful face, huge?
in Prospect Park, i see God
saw X's face fit to spill
off a Gildan, the kind we wear
with kin round the way, old photos
kissed by clouds, lurid as a bullhorn
to squeeze another drop of life
loudly out of the lost. X barks
then escapes the mourner's
hands like he's cheating
some untoward coda, fingers
on a speaker's knob coaxing
the cardinals to swallow their song.
the cherry blossoms today
blooming finally & one falls
with a hustler's grace, spins
then perches on my shoulder, remains
a moment, without a breeze
another petal, perhaps racing
to dismantle the distance, eddies
behind, pining, staccato
as X commands *stop.*
drop. lands, covering the scar
on my open palm, the other
blessing me one more bow
before coming to rest amongst the soil.

one side of Amy Winehouse's first post-rehab interview
after Eve L. Ewing & Hanif Abdurraqib

A: If you call lonely lucky.

A: Let's say demons could speak—they won't.

A: No, I still hear voices, but my higher power is between me & my higher power.

A: Whatever brings me close without burning. That's considered a high, yeah?

A: *A chorus of angels*—what rubbish. To watch over who?

A: They wouldn't want to watch.

A: Ain't they aware the devil is an angel?

A: Look, I never said that's who I sang for. I'll stretch any note til it breaks.

A: A song is a wordless thing that needs sayin'. Prayin' is for the bedroom.

A: Not that kind of prayer.

A: It's like water in a bowl your mouth can't reach.

A: To say I merely survived wouldn't do the moment justice.

A: Listen, I left a whole lot more than *money* on the table for a whole lot less.

A: By learning to be thankful for smaller miracles.

A: Not that small.

ouroboros   *soroboruo*

yesterday i chased two rabbits & both
escaped   only cruelty can come
 	
from such certainty   my melancholy
a creature shedding form   slim
 	
as a pepper seed   the marbled sighs
of a red-tailed hawk   sinking the sky
 	
if these fangs   fixed in my skin
could vanish   like common
 	
sense   all this prey
wouldn't be   so useless
 	
useless   you
know   hysterical
	hysterical you
	                                      know unless
	
	                                             i pray &
	vanish like common sense
	
	                     or fangs fixed to skin
	the sky singing the red-tailed hawk's
	
	        warble-cry sharp as pepper
	                spray a creature sheds
	
	from my melancholy its cruelty
	       crumbles under a century
	
	         of chastity there's nothing
	rabid to outrun i mean no one

on the gruesome death of honeybees, Sonny Rollins's sabbatical
& other incentives for loneliness

in the forest of my final exile
it was loneliness i learned

as darwinian—every storm growling

a kindly greeting
the black bear scampering

from my body's bouquet
like he'd been launched

by a nearsighted cannoneer.

the average human can
withstand one thousand

pangs per pound
from honeybees who dodge

our open hands
to pollinate blooms

we bring beloveds
& produce the air

we breathe. one sting

& the honeybee will rupture
its abdomen trying

to remove its weapon
heaving out instead

all its vital organs & well
i suppose this is merely

one of the softer risks of joy.

Sonny Rollins once took
a sabbatical for two years

between sandpipers
& the East River

blowing for no one
but the sky

& still found himself
sainted for ghosting

like a living Chinese finger trap.

now thousands of people dwell
in the building that bears

his name & stroll
The Bridge he made

famous, blissful as a fist of false pearls

so why can't i hum
through fields with lavender

in my hair without trampling
at least a few

snakes, without shaking

their rattles in my fists
like hospital bills.

do you hear that?
a zebra finch is dreaming

his songs to life. even in his sleep

he aches for the warmth
of another wing, parsing

pitch & timbre
prudently trimming

what won't dazzle a mate.

in the morning
melodies charm

even the most unmusical
passerby but sunrise

scares the daylights out of me

so i skulk the bridge
until the sky remembers

there are no mountains
in manhattan & makes the moon

marquee & i bleat an awful tone
a lone blue note

a breath i didn't know i was holding.

self-portrait as murmuration

imagine for instance a wounded starling
        the only reflection that greets you.
this is not a fun

        -house. my bathroom is aggressively plain,
holds all of my everyday essentials: reused Q-tips
        anti-frizz curl crème, little pink pills

that assure me they're non-habit
        forming. I don't know what to do
with my tenderness.

        suppose then a low-end
bass rattle that spits fissures
        through the floor. acclimation

becomes a necessary refrain. even Lady Day,
        gardenias adorning
her crown, found ways to summon evil

        while begging the moon
for clemency. how she sang *hunger* & meant
        penance, coaxed fear out of a sidewinder

with a few coiled moans. this too
        is the meeting
between predator & prey:

        a voice crackles, violence
swells in a swill
        of vodka. this season's starlings

will still take flight, arch & stretch
   their width to fill
a drinkable winter night. every feather knows

   what the sky knows, wings beating
like arrhythmia, a tangle of spiders' nests
   doted on while we sweep ashes

after the fire. I have a strange affection
   for creatures who crave mercy
but wind up instead with something like love.

   the best of us end here with limbs
so knotted you can't tell whose
   wrist you're pulling from the blue

-tipped blaze. in the bathroom mirror with cheekbones
   sharp & eyes like aimless weeds I meet
your face with the composure

   of a middle-distance runner. the birds bend
the wind to their will & somewhere
   in this bloom Lady sings the blues.

Acknowledgments

Grace & gratitude is owed & offered to the editors of the following journals where versions of these poems first appeared:

Alien Magazine: "on Lisa 'Left Eye' Lopes's stay in rehab & why i still sing to the dead"

American Poetry Journal: "last night i turned off the pilot light"

Black Warrior Review: "DMX teaches me how to pray"

The Boiler: "dirge for the last night of Eric Dolphy's life," pts. I & II and "the night of Dexter Gordon's comeback"

Cherry Tree: "through the front window of a haunted house, Amy Winehouse remembers the sky, a bruise"

Colorado Review: "slow singing & flower bringing"

The Commuter (Electric Literature): "i admit it i've never seen a falling star"

Denver Quarterly: "self-portrait as murmuration [my first memory is my four limbs]"

Epiphany Literary Journal: "arguing with my sponsor's ghost about the last place i saw him alive," "on her first sober tour Amy Winehouse plays nothing but ballads & refuses to sing anything in past tense," and "preparing for the next ice age while Amy Winehouse plays solitaire"

Gigantic Sequins: "aubade with Nina Simone who sang 'Sinnerman' & the whole world lost its balance" and "moral inventory [when i'm told people have more sex after funerals]"

Gordon Square Review: "on the gruesome death of honeybees, Sonny Rollins's sabbatical & other incentives for loneliness"

Guernica: "relapse dream"

Gulf Coast: "moral inventory [it's june i wouldn't know]"

Half Mystic: "spent gladiator #3"

Hayden's Ferry Review: "fragments from Amy Winehouse's stepwork journal," steps 1-3

Hobart: "my beloved forgets how to pray"

Iron Horse Literary Review: "withdrawal dream with Amy Winehouse chain-smoking in the dining hall of a rehabilitation center & plotting her escape"

The Journal: "& with every sunrise another reason to mourn"

Los Angeles Review: "on why Miles Davis quit playing ballads"

Massachusetts Review: "on Survivor's Guilt ending with 'Ruff Ryders' Anthem' by DMX"

Muzzle Magazine: "the summer after DMX died every rainfall felt like a benediction"

Newsletter (The Poetry Project): "delays & departures in an airport bar with Amy Winehouse"

Nashville Review: "unholy"

Northwest Review: "ghosts in the studio where Amy Winehouse records her comeback album"

Passages North: "nature retreat nocturne with Amy Winehouse"

Poetry Northwest: "ode to the seagull with what looks like a chicken bone in its beak but could be another seagull's leg for all i know"

Radar Poetry: "moral inventory sonnet featuring the serenity prayer"

The Recluse (The Poetry Project): "one side of Amy Winehouse's first post-rehab interview"

RHINO Poetry: "upon hearing Prince sing 'Purple Rain' at First Avenue in Minneapolis in 1983, i begin to understand my mother's love life"

The Rumpus: "grief"

The Rupture: "i am having so much fun without you"

Salt Hill Journal: "God loves everybody, don't remind me"

Southeast Review: "i think i'm finally ready to admit that i don't know the first thing about forgiveness"

Southern Indiana Review: "ode to the luna moth & my psychiatrist who warns me lithium will shorten my lifespan"

Sugar House Review: "all my attempts at meditation end in shouting matches with ghosts" and "that winter i wrote the same poem over & over"

Third Coast: "i can think of a dozen different ways to use that Motown 12" & none of them will sound as sweet as 'Dancing in the Street'"

THRUSH: "the profits of gravity"

Tupelo Quarterly: "fragments from Amy Winehouse's stepwork journal," steps 4-12

wildness: "self-portrait as murmuration [imagine, for instance, a wounded starling]"

Notes

During the writing & revising of *murmurations*, I was in communion & community with writers, musicians, beloveds, filmmakers, God, ghosts, angels, demons. I am not able to remember & source everyone; if I could, that Notes section would be endless. Thus, this is an incomplete & living list.

None of these poems would exist without Amy Winehouse, in particular the "fragments from Amy Winehouse's stepwork journal" series. These are found text poems whose only language source is the lyrics from Amy's two studio albums, *Frank* from 2003 & *Back to Black* from 2006.

This book wouldn't exist without the time, resources, ideas, and work of the following folx: John Darnielle, Ashna Ali, Cappadonna (from Wu-Tang Clan), Grace Paley, Sara Borjas, Julien Baker, John Murillo, Lil' Wayne & my cohorts in the Break Your Poems 2020 workshop led by Kaveh Akbar, Jay Deshpande, Malik Ameer Crumpler, Tariq Thompson, my cohorts in the Tin House 2020 Poetry Workshop led by Hanif Abdurraqib, Hanif Abdurraqib, Hala Alyan, Craig Finn, Angela Davis, Audre Lorde, Nina Simone, Peter Doherty, my grandmother, the Bellevue psychiatric center, Ziggy from *The Wire*, Raven Leilani, Jason Isbell, Matt Berninger, Christina Hatcher, Lynn Heron, George Cain, the *Wizard of Oz*, Martha & the Vandellas, Eric Tran, Ross Gay, José Olivarez, *Goodfellas*, Bruce Springsteen, Diannely Antigua, Jason Molina, Sarah Kay, Julian Randall, Lucia Berlin, Frasier, Shira Erlichman, Celina Su, Ilya Kaminsky, Franz Wright, Miles Davis, Bart Basile, Heather Christle, Mary Szybist, Paige Lewis, my sponsor, Traci Brimhall, Bonnie Raitt, Kevin Omen aka Kevo, Concrete Blonde, D.A., Nick Cave, Kanye West, Sudan Archives, Neko Case, Belle & Sebastian, the Only Ones, Ryan Adams, Elliott Smith, Conor Oberst, Rob Marvin, James Mercer, Stuart McLamb, Thom Yorke, Kristian Matsson, Ghinwa Jawhari, Jo Blair Cipriano, & Emma Bailey.

"spent gladiator #3" is an imagined sequel to the Mountain Goats songs "Amy aka Spent Gladiator" & "Spent Gladiator 2" from the 2012 album *Transcendental Youth*. It is about & dedicated to jazz bassist Jaco Pastorius, whose life was tragically cut short when he started a fight outside a club in Wilton Manors, Florida, & was beaten to death, an event spurred by a manic episode of bipolar.. He was 35. I wrote this poem a month before I was hospitalized from a suicide attempt & diagnosed with bipolar 1 myself.

"on Lisa 'Left Eye' Lopes's stay in rehab & why i still sing to the dead" is about & dedicated to Lopes, who was killed in a car accident while serving as a volunteer on a project building a children's development center in Honduras. She was 30.

"dirge for the last night of Eric Dolphy's life, parts 1 & 2" are for & about Dolphy, a jazz saxophonist who passed away from a diabetic coma when attending medical professionals assumed, based on pervading stereotypes of Black jazz musicians, that he'd overdosed on heroin. He was administered detoxification response meds & left to die. He was 36.

"relapse dream" was written for Robert James White.

"taste of cherries" is after Abbas Kiarostami & his film *Taste of Cherry* and borrows a line from "Demons" by The National.

"grief" is after Aracelis Girmay's poem "Here," as well as Leila Chatti's poem "The Rules."

"DMX teaches me how to pray" is for & after DMX. X was unable to overcome his demons & passed away in 2021. He was 50.

"arguing with my sponsor's ghost about the last place i saw him alive" borrows its title, entrance, & syntactical structure & rhythm from "The Last Place I Saw You Alive" by the Mountain Goats.

"the night of Dexter Gordon's comeback" use the phrase "I just walked into the room & they applauded," which is a line borrowed & slightly rephrased from a 1977 interview between Dexter Gordon & Chuck Berg.

"that winter i wrote the same poem over & over" is after Topaz Winters's "That Summer I Wrote the Same Poem Over & Over."

"on Whitney Houston's acceptance speech at the 2001 BET Awards & why i pray in the dark" refers to when Whitney accepted an award very visibly under the influence of cocaine & was dragged by the media. She was found dead from a drug-related drowning. She was 48.

"delays & departures in an airport bar with Amy Winehouse" is a bop, a poetic form created by Afaa Michael Weaver. Its refrain is borrowed from *Jazz* by Toni Morrison.

"slow singing & flower bringing" borrows its title from Erykah Badu's "Fall in Love (Your Funeral)" who herself borrowed the line from the Notorious B.I.G.'s "Warning."

"The Truth" was written for Scott Fobes. The form was borrowed & reshaped from Ocean Vuong's "Seventh Circle of Earth."

"the ocean isn't haunted it just holds our dead" was commissioned by Chase Elodia & originally appeared in his multimedia poetry project, *Walking in the City* & was written for Scott.

"on Survivor's Guilt ending with 'Ruff Ryders' Anthem' by DMX" was written for Scott & DMX & is after Anne Sexton's "The Truth the Dead Know." The line "is it not enough to sit somewhere / dark & see a beautiful face, huge?" is taken verbatim from a Mike Ginn tweet, with very generous & much appreciated permission.

"one side of Amy Winehouse's first post-rehab interview" borrows its form from Hanif & Eve L. Ewing. It borrows a line from "Mistaken for Strangers" by The National.

"on the gruesome death of honeybees, Sonny Rollins's sabbatical & other incentives for loneliness" refers to one of several sabbaticals jazz saxophonist Sonny Rollins took from the music scene to practice his instrument on the Williamsburg Bridge every day.

"self-portrait as murmuration" is in reference to Billie Holiday, who passed away from pulmonary edema & heart failure caused by cirrhosis of the liver. She was 44. The line "I don't know what to do with my tenderness" was taken from the most recent translation of Ingmar Bergman's film, *Persona*.

Gratitude

This isn't merely a series of thankyous to those who had a direct hand in this book's making; this is a litany of thankyous to anyone who has enriched my life, before or after its creation. I've woken up in the middle of the night to squeeze names onto this list. I would park my cart mid-aisle at the grocery store to scribble down initials & memories. It will ever be enough. I trust you know that if your name is missing from these pages, it isn't missing from my heart.

My students, first & foremost. You all push me to be better anytime I step foot into a classroom, onto a stage, out of my bed. My Brooklyn Poets students, you are my whole heart. Every drip. You are the reason I do this. My BMCC students, Evelyn, Paola, Edwin, Angie, Michael, Jorge, Deyshawn, Nicholas, John & Hugo Walsh, Laura Burhenn, Bree Bailey—your ferocious hearts are among the beatingest bloodiest I've ever witnessed.

My teachers. My mentors. My lights. Geoff Klock. You've taught me more about being an educator than anyone else. Kaveh Akbar. You're the poet I've tried to be since the day I read you, crying in a bookstore after a friend handed me *Calling a Wolf a Wolf* & said, "you need this." I did. I do. Hanif Abdurraqib. No one has taught me more about implementing community as a poet, sure, but more than that, as a person responsible for & accountable to more than myself. Hala Alyan. You have been a rock not just for me but for our whole community, Kan Yama Kan & beyond. After my mother's funeral, it was your backyard that I came to straight from the train station, all my bags in tow (emotional & physical). Celina Su. This book simply would not be without you. You took the 150 pages of poems I handed you & helped me shape them into this book. You taught me so much; I'm still peeling back the endless layers of your lessons.

My community. My communities. Brooklyn Poets. Kan Yama Kan. The Em-Dash Choir. My cohort at Tin House 2020. My people in Paris. The *Walking in the City* crew. The good folx at the Poetry Project, especially during my fellowship, including my fellow fellows. Anyone who has ever contributed to Word is Bond. I am better because of all y'all.

Ashna Ali. You are better than a sister. Your fierce devotion could power a small city. A planet. Because of you I'm better to my loved ones, I show up in all my essences to my communities, & there are few people in this galaxy I love as wildly as I love you. Megan Fernandes. You call me a real one more than you call me by my name, but you are truly the *realest*. Malik Ameer Crumpler. You may, in fact, be my favorite person on the planet.

Theo Legro. May our tongues be fast & full of shit talk, hearty laughs, & honored tears echo with our friendship into forever. Ghinwa Jawhari. We saw & knew each other almost immediately. Truly one of those Bogart & Rains walking into the sunset moments. Yusra Amjad. The fact we still keep such strong hooks in each other from opposite ends of the globe is a testament to how much I value you, your friendship, your honesty. Andrew Colarusso & Diana Cruz & Taylor & Co. My Cheers. There's nowhere else I'd rather lose 3-4 hours of my day & no one else I'd rather lose them with. r. kay. I know no heart as judiciously poetic as yours. You define leadership. You define community. You define hero to me.

The homies. Bart Basile, Becca Brennan Chiappone, Margaret Macaluso, Emma Bailey, Jose Morales Cruz, Christopher Lehr, XZen Marlow, River Ramos, Selena Spier, Hajri Aga, Mikayla Joy Dablan-Azony, Christina Hatcher, Michelle Hulan, Lisa Nguyen, Meara Levezow, Kimberleigh Costanzo, Noel Yu-Jen, Mason Eve, Kate Sweeney, Lara Atallah, Savannah Lauren, Rob Marvin, Kosta & Jamie Tzioumis, Chloe Johnson, Rachel Feldhaus, Nour MJ Hodeib, Leslie Donnenwirth, Jessy Edwards, Amanda Tarantino, Miro Crocco, Elizabeth Moylan, Yasmine Roukiaya, Areage Okab, Jaimee Vitolo Chiazza, Carine Gabrielle Gregorio, Lynn Heron, Danielle Reyes, Kerry Giangrande, Quinton Hinds, Sonia Park, Mary Benally, Victoria Viscusi, Richard Thomas Robinson, Robert Tahija, Myrsha Santos, & Peter Wolfgang.

Bella & Darius & Caro & Paula & Sofia & Hunter & Kayla & Jo & God I cannot even begin to name all of you but the entire Brooklyn Poets crews past & present. When someone speaks the word *family*, you are deadass the first ones I think of.

Sara Borjas, Adele Elise Williams, C. (Constantine Jones), Megan Pinto, Edgar Kunz, Topaz Winters, Hazem Fahmy, Tariq Thompson, DeeSoul Carson, Dante Clark, Alishya Almeida, Saba Keramati, Alyssa Froehling, Alexa Patrick, Sara Aziza, Gabrielle Bates, K. Iver, Chase Berggrun, Kamelya Omayma Youssef, Meryem Uzumcu, Seth Leeper, Amina Iro, Noor Hindi, Chen Chen, Jessica Abughattas, Lisa Hiton, sara mariah montijo, Diannely Antigua, Joy Priest, Keetje Kuipers, John Murillo, Nicole Sealey, Dalia Elhassan, Melissa Lozada-Olivia, Ladan Osman, Hafizah Geter, Jay Deshpande, Shira Erlichman, Angel Nafis, Zaina Arafat, Victoria Chang, Eugenia Leigh, Mahogany L. Browne, Daniella Toosie-Watson, Chase Elodia, Marissa Davis, Felice Belle, danilo machado, Ruth Awad, Ross Gay, Khadijah Queen, Zaina Alsous, Layli Long Soldier, Vanessa Angelica Villarreal, Tracy Fuad, José Olivarez, Divya Victor, Taylor Johnson, Paul Tran, Tarfia Faizullah, Kiran Bath, Sadia Hassan, Jonny Teklit, Natalye Childress, Ashni Dave, Ahmad Amireh,

Fatimah Asghar, Hannah Lillith Assadi, Karl Michael Iglesias, Sarah Ahmad, Arah Ko, Bryan Byrdlong, Stacey Park, Sara Mae, Alycia Pirmohamed, Nancy Miller Gomez, Aziza Barnes (bless your eternal soul), Jaz Sufi, Yahaira Galvez, C. Russell Price, Gabriel Don, Peter Torre, Ron Villanueva, Rishona Michael, William Oneal II, Sarah Admad, Laura Henriksen, Kyle Dacuyan, Alisha Mascarenhas, Rachelle Rahmé, Noelle de la Paz, imogen xtian smith, Stuti Sharma, Charlotte Abotsi, Stella Wong, Sarah Gisbon Tisdale, Kortney Morrow, Erin Noehre, Precious Musa, Alejandro Jimenez, Madeleine Cravens, Cynthia Tran, Kyle Liang, & Malvika Jolly.

Bringing it on home. KMA Sullivan. I could not have dreamt up a more caring, attentive, insightful, wide-eyed, tender, thoughtful editor. Thank you for giving this book a home & for welcoming me into the beautiful YesYes family: Devin, Karah, Gale, Jill, James. You've been my favorite press for years & you're my favorite press now. How lucky am I. Scott Fobes & Robert James White. I would trade every page in this book in a heartbeat to have you back. My analyst. You guided me toward a new way of emotional management, self-exploration, provided the tools I needed to dig deep & do my dirty work down there in the dark. God. For sparing my life more times than I probably deserved. For allowing me to see past 26 when every nurse & doctor in the Bellevue detox center said that medically I should be dead. Father Rafael J. Perez & the good folx at the Holy Family St. Thomas Aquinas Church in Brooklyn. I was in your pews when I learned that my mother had died. I thank God I was where I needed to be. My mother. You'll have been gone two years by the time this book sees light but you hang over each & every poem like the sky's fleeting stretch before nightfall. It'll take a whole book to even scratch our surface. We'll get to that in books #2 & #3. Brooklyn. The home that called me by my real name before I ever called her home.

& Riley. I wrote every poem in this book to momentarily distract the force of gravity & bend our orbits into one, & I didn't even know it until I met you by that lamp post one evening in May...

Also by YesYes Books

FICTION

The Nothing by Lauren Davis
Girls Like Me by Nina Packebush
Three Queerdos and a Baby by Nina Packebush

WRITING RESOURCES

Gathering Voices: Creating a Community-Based Poetry Workshop by Marty McConnell

FULL-LENGTH COLLECTIONS

Ugly Music by Diannely Antigua
Bone Language by Jamaica Baldwin
Cataloguing Pain by Allison Blevins
Strange Flowers by Bryan Byrdlong
What Runs Over by Kayleb Rae Candrilli
This, Sisyphus by Brandon Courtney
Salt Body Shimmer by Aricka Foreman
Gutter by Lauren Brazeal Garza
Forever War by Kate Gaskin
Inconsolable Objects by Nancy Miller Gomez
Ceremony of Sand by Rodney Gomez
Undoll by Tanya Grae
Loudest When Startled by luna rey hall
Everything Breaking / For Good by Matt Hart
40 WEEKS by Julia Kolchinsky
Sons of Achilles by Nabila Lovelace
Refusenik by Lynn Melnick
GOOD MORNING AMERICA I AM HUNGRY AND ON FIRE by jamie mortara
Born Backwards by Tanya Olson
a falling knife has no handle by Emily O'Neill
To Love An Island by Ana Portnoy Brimmer
Another Way to Split Water by Alycia Pirmohamed
Tell This to the Universe by Katie Prince
One God at a Time by Meghan Privitello
I'm So Fine: A List of Famous Men & What I Had On by Khadijah Queen
If the Future Is a Fetish by Sarah Sgro
Gilt by Raena Shirali
[insert] boy by Danez Smith
Say It Hurts by Lisa Summe
Hand Over Hand Over the Edge of the World by Patrick Swaney
Boat Burned by Kelly Grace Thomas
Helen Or My Hunger by Gale Marie Thompson
As She Appears by Shelley Wong

RECENT CHAPBOOK COLLECTIONS

Vinyl 45s

Exit Pastoral by Aidan Forster
Crown for the Girl Inside by Lisa Low
Phantasmagossip by Sara Mae
Year of the Sheep by Stacey Park
Scavenger by Jessica Lynn Suchon
Unmonstrous by John Allen Taylor
Giantess by Emily Vizzo

Blue Note Editions

Kissing Caskets by Mahogany L. Browne
One Above One Below: Positions & Lamentations by Gala Mukomolova
The Porch (As Sanctuary) by Jae Nichelle

www.ingramcontent.com/pod-product-compliance
Lightning Source LLC
Chambersburg PA
CBHW080409170426
43193CB00016B/2867